Marie Curie

Published by Roaring Brook Press
Roaring Brook Press is a division of Holtzbrinck Publishing Holdings Limited Partnership
175 Fifth Avenue, New York, NY 10010
mackids.com

Library of Congress Control Number: 2017957908
ISBN 978-1-250-16615-9

Our books may be purchased in bulk for promotional, educational, or business use. Please contact your
local bookseller or the Macmillan Corporate and Premium Sales Department at (800) 221–7945 ext. 5442
or by e–mail at MacmillanSpecialMarkets@macmillan.com.

First published in France in 2015 by Quelle Histoire, Paris
First U.S. edition, 2018

Text: Patricia Crété
Translation: Catherine Nolan
Illustrations: Bruno Wennagel, Mathieu Ferret

Printed in China by RR Donnelley Asia Printing Solutions Ltd., Dongguan City, Guangdong Province

10 9 8 7 6 5 4 3 2 1

Marie Curie

Roaring Brook Press
New York

Childhood in Poland

Marie Curie was a brilliant scientist. She was born Maria Skłodowska in Poland in 1867.

Her father was a math and science professor and her mother was a teacher. Young Maria always ranked at the top of her class in school. But girls were not allowed to go to college in Poland. So in 1891, Maria moved to France.

———

1867–1891

Studies in Paris

Maria became a student at the Sorbonne University in Paris. She started calling herself Marie, which sounded more French than Maria.

Marie studied a kind of science called physics. She was most interested in elements, the building blocks that make up all things.

She worked hard and earned two degrees: one in physics and another in math.

———

1891–1894

Falling in Love

Marie had planned to go back to Poland when she finished school. But then she met another scientist, named Pierre Curie. They fell in love!

Marie and Pierre got married in 1895. One of their wedding gifts was a pair of bicycles. They rode them everywhere.

Two years later, they had a daughter, Irène. Irène would grow up to be a scientist, just like her parents.

———

1895–1898

New Elements

Marie and Pierre set up a lab so they could do research. The lab wasn't fancy. One visitor said it looked like a potato cellar!

Working together, they discovered two new elements. They named them polonium and radium.

These elements gave off rays of energy called radiation. Before long, the Curies were experts in the study of radiation.

———

1898–1903

Nobel Prize

In 1903, Marie and Pierre won a prize for their work. It was the Nobel Prize in Physics—the biggest award in the field. Marie was the first woman ever to win it!

Later, Marie would win the Nobel Prize again, making her the first person in history to win it twice.

_____

1903

Professor Curie

Life was good for the Curies. Pierre became a professor at the Sorbonne University. Marie gave birth to their second daughter, Ève.

Then something awful happened. Pierre was hit by a horse-drawn cart and killed.

Marie was terribly sad. But she stayed strong. When the university asked her to take over Pierre's job, she said yes. She became the Sorbonne's first female professor.

———

1906

Radiation

Marie kept up her work on radiation, too. Radiation turned out to be a big help in the field of medicine. X-ray machines made it possible to take pictures of people's insides. Doctors could check the images for broken bones and other problems.

————

1909–1914

"Little Curies"

In 1914, World War I broke out. A lot of soldiers were wounded on the battlefield. It was hard to get them to the hospital for X-rays.

Marie had an idea. She would take the X-ray equipment to the battlefield instead! She set up special ambulances with X-ray machines inside. The army called the vehicles "Little Curies."

Marie got her driver's license so she could drive the ambulances herself. Her daughter Irène went with her. They helped save many wounded people during the war.

1914–1918

Treasure

After the war, Marie faced a problem. She was running out of radium. She needed more so she could keep studying radiation.

Marie knew she could get radium at a special factory in America. But it was very expensive. One tiny gram cost $100,000! How would she ever afford it?

A group of American women decided to help. They raised the money and gave it to Marie.

In the spring of 1921, Marie took a ship to the United States and picked up a gram of radium. It was tucked in a beautiful wooden box, like a treasure.

———

1921

Last Years

Marie went back to France. She worked with radiation for many more years.

No one knew it at the time, but radiation can be dangerous. A little of it—enough for an X-ray—is fine. But being around radiation for so long made Marie very sick. She died on July 4, 1934.

In 1995, Marie and Pierre Curie received a great honor. Their coffins were moved to the Pantheon in Paris, the resting place of France's heroes.

———

1934

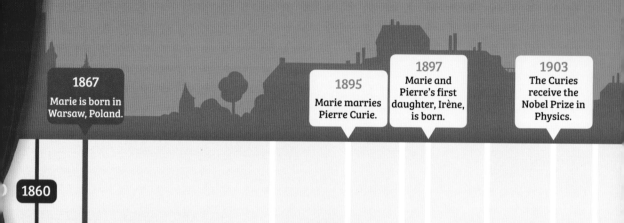

1867
Marie is born in Warsaw, Poland.

1860

1895
Marie marries Pierre Curie.

1897
Marie and Pierre's first daughter, Irène, is born.

1903
The Curies receive the Nobel Prize in Physics.

1891
She enrolls at the Sorbonne University and takes the name Marie.

1897
Marie begins her thesis on radiation produced by the element uranium.

1898
Marie and Pierre discover radium.

1906
Pierre dies.

1906
Marie becomes a science professor.

1911
Marie receives the Nobel Prize in Chemistry.

1918
Marie heads a lab at the Radium Institute.

1921
She travels to the U.S. to buy radium.

1934
Marie dies in France.

1995
The Curies' coffins are moved to the Pantheon.

2011
The 100th anniversary of Marie's second Nobel Prize. France names it the "Marie Curie Year."

2018

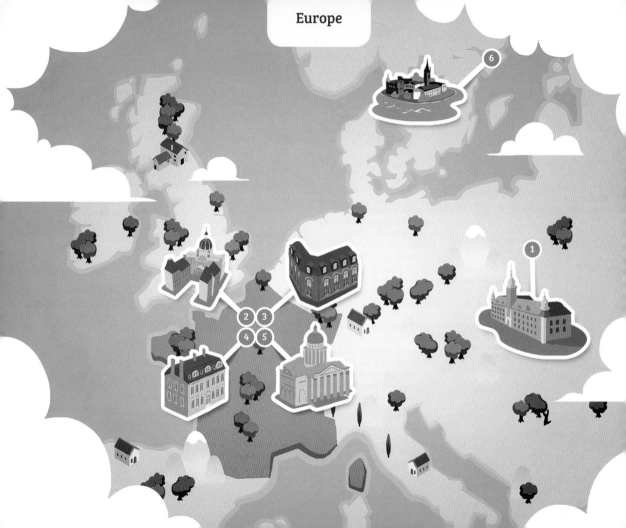

Europe

1 Warsaw, Poland

The house where Marie Curie was born is now a museum that honors her.

2 Sorbonne University, Paris, France

Marie was both a student and a professor here.

3 The College of Industrial Physics and Chemistry, Paris, France

Marie and Pierre did some of their research here.

4 Curie Institute, Paris, France

Marie ran a lab at this institute, which was first called the Radium Institute. It's an important center for cancer research and treatment.

5 The Pantheon, Paris, France

France's national heroes are laid to rest here. Marie is one of only a few women to be buried at the Pantheon.

6 Stockholm, Sweden

The Nobel Prize ceremony is held here, at the town hall.

People to Know

Pierre Curie
(1859–1906)
Pierre was Marie's husband and work partner. He won the Nobel Prize with Marie in 1903.

Irène Joliot-Curie
(1897–1956)
Pierre and Marie's older daughter followed in her parents' footsteps and became a scientist. She won a Nobel Prize in 1935.

Émile Roux
(1853–1933)
This doctor started the Radium Institute to treat cancer patients using radiation. The institute was later renamed the Curie Institute.

Antoine Béclère
(1856–1939)
Antoine was in charge of the French army's X-ray services during World War I. He supported Marie and her "Little Curies."

....

Girls were not allowed to go to college in Poland. For a while, Marie went to a "floating" school—a secret school that moved from place to place so that the police wouldn't find it.

....

Marie could have received a patent for her discoveries. Then other scientists would have had to pay to use her research. But Marie refused. She wanted other scientists to use her research for free.

....

Pierre and Marie did not know how dangerous radiation could be. Their lab notes and other belongings are not safe to touch, even today. They give off too much radiation.

....

Marie was extremely shy. During her visit to the U.S. in 1921, she wore a sling on her arm. Her arm wasn't really broken. She just wanted a break from shaking people's hands!

Available Now

 Muhammad Ali

 Neil Armstrong

 Blackbeard

 Coco Chanel

 Charlie Chaplin

 Cleopatra

 Marie Curie

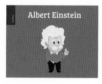 Albert Einstein

 Abraham Lincoln

 Nelson Mandela

 Isaac Newton

 Rosa Parks

Coming Soon

 Anne Frank

 Gandhi

 Frida Kahlo

 Martin Luther King, Jr.